Meditating on God's Word

The Key to Successful Christian Living

Meditating

on

God's Word

The Key to Successful Christian Living

Samuel Brown

© 2004 by Samuel Brown. All rights reserved

Printed in the United States of America

No part of this publication may be reproduced, stored in a retrieval system, or transmitted in any way by any means-electronic, mechanical, photocopy, recording, or otherwise-without the prior permission of the copyright holder, except as provided by USA copyright law

Scriptures references are taken from the King James Version of the Bible.

Published by:
Ufomadu Consulting & Publishing
P.O. Box 746
Selma, AL 36702-0746

ISBN 0-9754197-1-4
Library of Congress Catalog Card Number: 2004097481

Table of Contents

Dedication 7
Acknowledgement 9
Introduction 13
Chapter 1 How it All Began 21
Chapter 2 The Power of Meditation 39
Chapter 3 Meditation Causes You to See a Picture 51
Chapter 4 Keeping Your Mouth Full of God's Word 61
Chapter 5 Meditation Keys 69

Dedication

Dedicated to my father, Horne Brown, Sr., who passed in May 1987. My father taught me the value of good family relationships. He also taught me how to provide for my family. Because of his great example as a father and provider, he deserves the credit for the man I have become. Thank you, Daddy.

Acknowledgements

My Pastor, Effell Williams Sr.; who has been the perfect example of a man of God. My connection to him and the Tabernacle of Praise ministry has allowed that same anointing to manifest itself in my life.

My mother, Ruby Brown, whom I can never repay for doing a great job in raising me in the way of the Lord. Mother, I love you with all my heart.

Minister Fred Ishman, who encouraged me to write when I did not think I was able. Thank you Fred for your support.

My wonderful Mother-in-Law, Bobbie Singleton, who helped me in my writing. Thanks for being such a great supporter.

Introduction

Those of us who believe in and mediate on God's word need to be aware that we are in a season of abundance. It is very important that we prepare ourselves spiritually and mentally for this movement of the Spirit. Our minds must be transformed by the word of God. What we think is a very important key to what we receive.

> For as he think in his heart,
> so is he… Proverb 23:7 (KJV)

It is important that we seek God in this hour like never before. This is the season and time for prosperity like the body of Christ has never seen. Everything is in place. All we have to do is follow the plan of God. Someone might ask, "What is God's plan?" God's word- the Bible – clearly defines and outlines His plan.

God's plan and our lives exist together. His thoughts of us are always filled with loving kindness: "For I know the thoughts I think toward you, saith the Lord, thoughts of peace and not of evil"...(Jer 29:10). Our heavenly Father has a plan for our lives: "To give [us] an expected end and hope for [our] final outcome" (Jer 29:11).

The Bible is the only true source of proof on God's plan for our lives. However, we must learn how God's plan is revealed to us and manifested through us. God's word doesn't just happen in our lives. We must do our part as He commanded.
Deuteronomy 28:1-2 states, "And it shall come to pass if thou shalt hearken diligently unto the voice of the Lord thy God, to observe and to do all His commandments, which I command thee this day, that the Lord thy God will set thee on high above all nations of the earth: "And all these blessings shall come on thee,

and overtake thee. If thou shalt hearken unto the voice of the Lord thy God."

Obedience is the most important thing in our Christian walk. We cannot add anything to His word nor can we take anything away. Let us not remain idle in our hearing. So let's be doers and not hearers only...." (James 1:22).

We cannot pick out the part of His word that we want to obey. We must walk according to all that is written. This means that we must love our enemies, bless them that curse us, do good to them that hate us and pray for them which despitefully use and persecute us (Matthew 5:44, KJV). We must walk according to all that is written:

> Only be thou strong and very courageous,
> that thou mayest observe to do according

> to all the law, which Moses my servant commanded thee: turn not from it to the right hand or to the left, that thou mayest prosper whithersoever thou goest.
> Joshua 1:7 (KJV)

It was never God's plan for the body of Christ to live in lack. When God created man and placed him in the garden, He made provisions for man's every need and desire in the garden.

Imagine a life where there is no lack. Imagine a place of peace and being in complete fellowship with the Creator of the universe. Imagine living in a land with no sickness, sadness or sorrow. Indeed, this was God's plan, but man gave it up when he chose to mediate on a lie rather than on the truth.

> Blessed is the man that walketh
> not in the counsel of the ungodly,
> nor standeth in the way of sinners,
> nor sitteth in the seat of the scornful.
> but his delight is in the law of the
> Lord; and in His law doth he mediate
> day and night
>   Psalm 1:1-2
> KJV

Clearly we must believe the report of the Great Planner. Whose report will you believe? Everything else is a lie from the pit of hell. Our focus must be on God's word. Satan would like for us to focus on what we see rather than on God's word. His plan (Satan) is to make us believe our conditions and circumstances. He wants us to meditate on his lies and deception. Every time we are at our weakest point, Satan shows up to trouble our minds with lies. Satan will use whatever methods he can to get us to meditate on deceptions rather than on God's word. We must fight Satan's deceptions with the knowledge of God's word:

> Ye are of your father the devil, and the lust of your father you will do. He was a murderer from the beginning, and abode not in the truth, because there is no truth in him. When he speak a lie, he speaketh of his own: for he is a liar and the father of it.
> John 8:44 KJV

It is time for us to open our eyes and see ourselves as God does. Then we can see clearly the enemy and his traps for our lives. The only way that our eyes can become open is by renewing our mind with constant meditation on the word of God. Through meditation on His word, we can enter into a new day with a different outlook, knowing that we are part of God's divine plan.

Chapter 1

How It All Began

Childhood is perhaps the most memorable and exciting period in life. Life was slow, sweet, and easy because our innocence made us unaware of the many problems our parents faced- problems that we would eventually face as well. But even in childhood, many youths- in spite of innocence- experience difficult times. Many young people are born with God's call on their lives:

> Before I formed thee in the
> belly I knew thee; and before
> thou comest forth out of the
> womb I sanctified thee, and
> I ordained thee a prophet
> unto the nations
> Jeremiah 1:5 KJV

Satan's plan, however, is to destroy the called before God's plan is ever recognized and achieved. It is the one reason for his existence in our lives. "The thief cometh to kill, steal and destroy" John 10:10.

I grew up in a small town that only consisted of a few hundred people. My neighborhood was very small, and everyone that lived there were relatives. Everybody trusted each other. There were no indications why a child couldn't go any where in the neighborhood and not feel safe.

My childhood was very fun. I can remember riding my bike all through the neighborhood. Remember, everyone who lived there were relatives, so what could go wrong? However, something did go wrong.

At the age of six, I can remember spending a lot of time at my cousin's house. I didn't understand what was happening. It all started out as fun and games, but something terrible happened. This thing entangled me for years; I thought I would never break free.

One day my cousin and I were alone in the house and she made me have sex with her. I didn't understand what was going on then, but Satan did. This was his time to destroy the call that he recognized on my life. This went on for weeks, and no one ever knew.

How could a six-year-old child explain this to anyone? What would I say? At that time, I didn't think it was wrong. She told me that it was fine. So I continued to do what she requested of me, not knowing what I was being introduced to.

Eventually, it all came to a stop, but the memories kept going in my mind. I grew up with a lust problem and dealing with a constant fight of all kinds of immoral desires. At the ages of ten and eleven, most children would be satisfied with just bike riding, but I was more interested in girls.

When I was in the fourth grade, I can remember trying to put my hands in a girl's pants. The spirits of lust and immorality were trying to invade my life. Satan's plan was indeed working. As I grew older, I became curious about the female body parts. In my mind, I would try to imagine what the female body parts looked like. My curiosity grew stronger and stronger.

During my early teens, I was really trying hard to experience sex. I couldn't understand what was happening to me. My body was going through some serious changes.

By the time I was in the eighth grade my mother and sister purchased satellite dish. I did not completely understand the possibilities of this new technology. My friend, whose name was Terry, told me about all the channels. Later he introduced me to the playboy channel. Late at night when everyone was asleep, I would put the television on the playboy channel. This is what I was curious about. My love for it grew more and more.

During my ninth grade year, my problems grew worse. I really wanted to have sex because everyone was talking about it. Everyone was doing it-except me- I thought.

During one school activity, which was the Halloween Carnival. I tried to have sex in the scary house exhibit. My attempt was unsuccessful but I continued my pursuit on a daily basis.

When I turned sixteen in my tenth grade year my mission was accomplished. I got my chance at sex. The girl was older and very promiscuous. Little did I know that the spirit of whoredom was invading my life. I became one with a harlot.

> What? Know ye not that he which is joined to harlot is one body? For two saith he, shall be one flesh.
> 1 Corinthians 6:16 KJV

In August of 1987, I began my eleventh grade year. What a fun year it was. I was popular and a good basketball player. All the girls loved me for some strange reason and some knew I didn't really care for them. Satan was sending them my way. I took advantage of all my opportunities to have sex. It didn't really matter about the place. The school bathroom was just an example of how bad I really had it.

After my eleventh grade year, basketball caused my name to spread all over the county. During the summer before my twelfth grade year, I found a good paying job. With the money that I earned, I was able to purchase all of the popular brand name clothing. I would receive compliments from my peers and teachers. Everything was falling into place just as I hoped.

Our basketball season started in November 1989. Keith High Bears were on a mission. We were on a roll, I thought. We were almost unbeatable and teams feared us. I was the center of attraction, and I loved it.

There were times when I would sit and think about what I had seen on the playboy channel. Who would I find to fulfill these desires? During this time, I was not in the church and had no relationship with God. I had no conviction of any sort. I was proud and quite happy about what I was doing. My mind was constantly on doing wrong.

During this time I had no idea of what I was doing. Now I can clearly see how Satan took what I meditated on and made it a reality in my life. What you meditate on will eventually manifest itself in your life. This was just the beginning of many difficult times throughout the years of my life.

After I graduated from high school and went off to college, things only got worse. For me, college became a place of pleasure and good times. Unlike high school, there was no one to make me attend classes. It was a personal choice. When you are a college athlete some administrators really are not concerned with class attendance, just as long you do enough to get through them. I wasted a lot of valuable years trying to live out a fantasy, which eventually lead me to withdrawing from school.

Life became difficult. I was having fun but I had no peace. My Lifestyle made me happy, but I had no real joy. You see my friend, you can be doing what you like and still not like what you are doing. This is what Paul was expressing in the book of Romans:

> For I do not understand my own action [I am baffled, bewildered]. I do not practice or accomplish what I wish, but I do the very thing that I loathe [which my moral instinct condemns]
> Romans 7:15 AMP

Paul's greatest struggle was in his own mind. At some point in time, Paul allowed things to enter his mind and these things later came back to haunt him. Notice carefully to his statement in Romans 7:23: "But I see another law in my members warring against the law of my mind, and bringing me into captivity to the law of sin which is in my members."

Here is an example of what Paul was encountering. I'm sure you have seen a cartoon where an angel would appear on the character's shoulder and a picture of the devil on the other. The angel would always remind the character to do the right thing. On the other hand, the devil would always try to persuade the character to do what was wrong. Even when Paul desired to do good, evil was present with him. First, we must defeat the enemy (Satan) in our minds. Until our minds are free, we will never be free. This can began by renewing your mind in God's word and meditating on His word. Remember that the problem is not in your checkbook. The problem is in your thinking. If you break the bondage of poverty in your mind you can break it in your checkbook, but you must drive the enemy out of your mind first. For as he thinketh in his heart so is he (Proverb 23:7).

After years of trying to do my own thing, I gave my life to Christ in 1992. My family found a Bible-believing church in Selma, Alabama. This church gave me a good foundation to build on. The images I fought so hard to get away from were finally leaving. I started to renew my mind in God's word. The light had finally come on; it's all over.

Looking at some of my past failures, I can clearly see how Satan deceived me through the control of my mind. As a matter of fact, every time I found myself yielding to sin, it was through the thought process. I struggled for years, trying to overcome the hold of the enemy.

I was frustrated and felt like a failure, unable to recognize the scheme of the enemy. My church attendance was nearly perfect. I was present at every program, -Bible study, and Sunday morning service. In addition, my pastor taught me how to be free through the word, but I was still falling into Satan's traps. When will this all end I asked myself? Miraculously, I learned about the power of mediation.

The word *meditate* means to mentally envision. It also means to think, chew and munch on a particular thing with all your time and energy until you are consumed by it. Ultimately it becomes your main focus on a daily basis. When you wake up in the morning it's what you think about. This is what God meant when He told us to mediate day and night (Joshua 1, KJV).

Many of God's people are being snared by the same methods and tricks. Many are asking the same question I once asked: Why do I keep falling to Satan and his plan? The answer to this question maybe diverse and complicated; however, it begins with a thought pattern.

Finally, my Brethren, whatsoever things are true, whatsoever things are honest, whatsoever things are just, whatsoever things are pure, whatsoever things are lovely, whatsoever things are of a good report; if there be any virtue, and if there be any praise, meditate on these things.

Philippians 4:8, NKJV

The book of Philippians instructs us to meditate on the things that are true, honest, just, and pure. When Satan controls our thought processes, we focus on the things that are false, dishonest, wrong, and unclean. It is very important to study a portion of God's word and meditate on that word daily, 'For the word of the Lord is right; and all His works are done in truth." Satan's deceptions can be revealed; his hold on our minds can be destroyed through daily meditation on God's word.

> I beseech you therefore, brethren by the mercy of God, that you present your bodies a living sacrifice, holy, acceptable to God, which is reasonable service. And be not conformed to this world; but be ye transformed by the renewing of your mind, that you may prove what is that good, and acceptable, and perfect will of God.
>
> Romans 12:1-2 KJV

During the period of some of my greatest difficulties, I accepted God's call to preach and minister the Gospel. This acceptance created new problems because other people now looked to me for guidance and correction. My every thought was filled with the fear that my own imperfections would be revealed. Through meditation on God's word, I realized that God was aware of my secret conflicts:

> Thou knowest my downsitting and my uprising, thou understandest my thoughts afar off.
> Thou compassest my path and my lying down, and art acquainted with all my ways.
> For there is not a word in my tongue but, lo O Lord, thou knowest it all together.
> Psalm 139: 2-4 KJV

What we meditate on will eventually manifest itself in our lives. My past life was living proof of this. Satan had it all planned. He constantly fed and troubled my mind with all kinds of ungodly images. Consider this carefully my friend: If you meditate on Satan's ideas long enough, you will eventually act on them.

Remember, Satan cannot read our minds. He only knows what we are thinking based on our words and actions. What we do and say is the key to the enemy's strategy. If we say we can't when God's word says that we can, this proves that we are accepting Satan's lies. We cannot resist Satan by our efforts alone. But with God's help, we can defeat the enemy, knowing that 'I can do all things through Christ which strengtheneth me (Philippians 4:13).

The turning point in my life began when I changed my thinking pattern. I began to renew my mind with the word of God. My spiritual vocabulary had a tremendous turn around. Words began to come out of my mouth like this: "I'm more than a conqueror" (Romans 8:37); "No weapon formed against me shall prosper" (Isaiah 54:17); "I can do all things through Christ that strengthens me" (Philippians 4:13).

There is a reason why I chose to share these personal experiences with you. In today's social environment, people from all age groups can become enslaved by the trappings of unacceptable, immoral behaviors. For example, sex is one of the many enterprises that Satan uses to entrap those who do not know the comfort and wisdom that can be found in God's word. According to God sex is a sacred act; it is meant to be shared between a husband and wife. It is the ultimate expression of love between two people. However, sexual prowess is not our entire purpose in life. We must use our time searching for God's purpose in our lives- and when we find it- we will find true fulfillment. We must seek God first, and everything will follow its place of order in our lives.

The following chapters are designed to give you sources of wisdom to which you may turn for help in battling any addiction and life's everyday problems. These sources were very useful in setting me free, and I draw strength from them daily. Read them, re-read them, and meditate on their meanings. I hope you find the same freedom and strength and that I have found as you continue to come closer to God's purpose for your life.

Chapter 2

The Power of Meditation

In Joshua 1:8 God said something that was very powerful and profound. Joshua was given specific instructions that would put him right into the land of promise. Moses had died, and it was Joshua's responsibility to get the people into the Promised Land. Joshua became fearful at the great task that was put before him. However, God encouraged him to be strong and courageous.

> Only be thou strong and very courageous, that thou may observe to do according to all the law, which Moses my servant command thee…
> Joshua 1:7

Sometimes in our lives we become fearful when we look at our circumstances. It is easy to believe God when we have everything we need to complete a particular assignment, but what happen when God commands us to do something that is bigger or beyond what we have? Our minds take stock of our resources, and the task seems totally impossible. This is the time we should seek the face of God and renew our minds according to what He has said concerning us.

What were the instructions Joshua received from God? It was simply this: to meditate day and night. Remember that the word meditate means to mentally envision. Spend your time, Joshua, focusing on my word instead of the task that is ahead of you. There is no one or nothing that can stop you from entering into the Promised Land if you follow this commandment. Meditate on my word.

> There shall not any man
> be able to stand before
> thee all the day of thy life;
> as I was with my servant
> Moses so will I be with thee;
> I will not fail thee, nor forsake thee
>
> Joshua 1:5 KJV

God assured Joshua that man didn't have the power or resources to stop him from receiving what had been promised. We can not allow ourselves to be intimidated by man, or circumstances because the greater power lives on the inside of us. "As I was with Moses so will I be with thee";... Joshua 1:5.

> What shall we then say to
> these things? If God be for us,
> who can be against us?
> Romans 8:31 KJV

Why would the almighty God tell Joshua to meditate day and night, if it wasn't an important part of his success? God knew that if he could get Joshua to meditate on the promise long enough, eventually he would believe it. "Spend your time thinking on the promise," God said. "Keep it before your eyes, put it in your mind and say it with your mouth. I will not fail thee…" (Joshua 1:5)

Then Joshua commanded the people saying, "Pass through the host, and command the people, saying prepare you victuals: for within three days ye shall pass over this Jordan… to go in to possess the land, which the Lord your God giveth you to possess it.
Joshua 1:11

Now we see a man who was willing to put aside all his fears and now convinced that he is able to enter in and possess the land of promise. Joshua had a new outlook on the situation all because of constant meditation. Now the people were willing to follow Joshua. They now saw a man who was full of faith and determination. Spiritual meditation is contagious; all around you are infected by it. The way we think can have a positive or negative influence in the life of others.

> And they answered Joshua, saying
> All that thou command us we will do
> And withersoever thou sendest us
> we will go.
> According as we hearkened unto

> Moses in all things, so will we hearken
> Unto thee: only the Lord thy God be with
> Thee as he was with Moses.

Joshua 1: 16-17

Can you now see the power of meditating of God's word? The results are very clear. If we spend our time and energy meditating on the promise long enough, it will come to pass in our lives. Do not misunderstand me, my friend. I'm not saying that we do not have to do anything else except think on God's word and every promise will come to pass in your life. However, meditating on God's word starts the transformation- which enables you to believe that you can do anything His word says; YOU CAN DO! Satan knows the power of positive meditation. This is the reason why he

(Satan) tries to get you to think on the negatives.

    Yet, even after giving my life to Jesus Christ, I still struggled for years with my past. I just couldn't seem to break free in my mind. Every moment that I was alone, the enemy would torment me with all kinds of thoughts. Once again, it seemed as if I was being pulled back.
    For years I was living a secret life. I was in the church, but my mind seem to be else where. I was hiding the fact that I still had a lot of ungodly desires even thought I was born again. So once again I began to act on all those things, and it all came out.

> For there is nothing covered,
> that shall not be revealed;
> neither hid, that shall not
> be known. Therefore

whatsoever ye have spoken
in darkness shall be heard
in the light; and that
which ye have spoken in
the ear in closets shall be
proclaimed upon the housetops
Luke 12 2:3

Thinking the wrong thoughts caused me to have the wrong desires. At first, the desires and thought seemed to be innocent. They later came back to haunt me. If we meditate on God's word, our lives will be prosperous and successful. If we become consumed by our desires and the lies of Satan, we will live a defeated and unfulfilled life.

For to be carnally minded is death; but to be spiritually minded is life and peace

Romans 8:6 KJV

According to high blood pressure researchers over 5,000 students in South Carolina were screened and 156 had high blood pressure. Half of that group would receive fifteen minutes of positive meditation sessions daily. The other half-a control group-were places in health education classes. All students wore blood pressure monitors 24 hours a day. The students who were places in the control group had no reduction in their blood pressure, according to the study in the American Journal of Hypertension. Besides reducing their blood pressure, students who received fifteen minutes daily positive meditation had lower rates of absenteeism, school rule violations and suspensions than those in the control group. If positive meditation helped students to lower their blood pressure, what would happen if we spend one hour a day meditating on God's word?

Spend your time meditating on the positive things in life. For example, you can start by focusing on your purpose. Ask yourself why are you here. Get deeper in God's word and find out more about His will for your life. You and I were put here to make a difference in someone else's life. Let's not spend all of our time focusing on ourselves. We can avoid the traps and pitfalls of life if we would just follow God's word. Meditate on these thoughts and ideas today, and let it be a new beginning for you.

Brethren, I count not myself to have apprehended: but this one thing I do, forgetting those things which are behind,
and reaching forth unto those things which
are before,
I press toward the mark for the Prize

of the high calling of God in Christ Jesus.
Philippians 3: 13-14 KJV

Chapter 3
Meditation Allows You to See a Picture

Our God is the awesome God, all knowing and powerful. There is nothing that is hidden from him. He never makes mistakes nor does He need corrections. Whatever He speaks comes to pass, and no problem is too big for him. Trouble never catches Him off guard. The Bible states that He neither slumbers nor sleep.

Everything is subject to Him whether it is in the Heavens, Earth, or beneath. He is the Alpha and the Omega, the beginning, and the end. (Revelation 1:8).

God's word is very clear when it comes to our mental states. He not only tells us what to think, but how often. What we think is what we'll see. If you meditate on the truth long enough you'll see the real picture. The real picture is that you are more than a conqueror. You're blessed in the field and blessed in the city. Wealth and riches are a part of the covenant that you have with God. You have the favor of the Lord. Envision God's favor on your life. Meditate on this picture, and take hold of it right now!!

In Joshua, chapter one, it states: 'that thou mayest observe to do according to all that is written therein." Read this three times before going any further. Can you see now what God was trying to reveal to Joshua? The revelation is this: Not only will meditation cause you to see God's will for your life, but it will also allow you to do accomplish all that's written. This is God's purpose when he allows you to observe something or to envision a particular thing. God doesn't just want you to see it without achieving it, but in order to see the picture that God is trying to reveal, you must meditate on His word. Never spend your time meditating on the negative opinions of others.

Satan will use whatever he can to get you to spend your time focusing on something else other than God's word. Why is this, my friend? Because anything else other than God's word will reveal a false picture and cause you to do contrary to God's law:

> The secret thing belong unto the Lord our God; but those things which are revealed belong unto us and our children forever, that we may do all the word of this law
>
> Deuteronomy 29:29

Let's look a little deeper at what meditation will cause you to see. Has there ever been a time in your Christian walk when Satan came to you and whispered a lie? During this time the enemy was so subtle in doing this, you weren't aware of his plan and purpose. You probably heard him say something like this: where you are and the situation you are in will never change. You'll always remain broke, busted and disgusted the rest of your life. Why would Satan tell you this? His plan (Satan) is to get you to see yourself according to what he has told you but, this is not the truth. The truth about your situation is: For you know the grace of our Lord Jesus Christ, that, though He was rich yet for your sake He became poor, that ye through His poverty might be rich (2 Corinthians 8:9).

You have a right according to God's word to have riches. Meditate on this truth, and picture yourself walking and living in a wealthy place.

Observation is what Satan uses to discourage us but we do not walk by what we see, we walk by faith.

While we look not at the things which are seen, but at the things which are not seen. For the things which are seen are temporal; but the things which are not seen are eternal

2 Corinthians 4:18 KJV

Moses received a command from the Lord. God said to him "send thou men, that they may search the land of Canaan.." (Numbers, 13:2). After searching the land as Moses instructed, they brought back an evil report. The men said "we are not able to go up against the people; for they are stronger than we." (Number 13:31). Caleb, on the other hand, had a different attitude about the land. He didn't let what he had observed discourage what had been revealed to him by God. Moses sent twelve men to spy out the land, but only two had a good report. Could it be that the ten decide to focus on what they saw, rather than meditating on the promise, which was given by God? If we decide to meditate on the giants in our lives this will be the picture that we will see. "And we were in our own sight as grasshopper and we are in their sight (Numbers 13:33)

Notice something very important in Numbers 13:33. It was not the giants who saw them as grasshoppers; it was in their own eyes that they viewed themselves as being less than what was told to them by God. Most of the time it is not the problem that we face that hinders us. The problem lies in how we see ourselves in relation to the problem. We must meditate on this truth: No weapon formed against me shall prosper (Isaiah 54:17).

Let's look at Abraham, the father of faith. Abraham received a promise from God that he would have a son. This was given to a man and woman who were past child bearing. Sarah, his wife, thought that this was impossible. "Therefore Sarah laughed within herself, saying, after I am waxed old shall I have pleasure, my lord being old (Genesis 18:12). This was impossible to men, but with God all things are possible. The Bible states that Abraham did not consider his own body now dead, when he was about a hundred years old neither yet the deadness of Sarah's womb (Romans 4:19).

Why consider what you are facing. God is greater than anything you face. Meditate on His word and watch God work in your life.

If you meditate on the things of God and His word, you can always see yourself overcoming whatever you are facing. The reason why so many people in the body of Christ cannot get out of situations they are in is because they cannot mentally envision freedom. When we meditate on God's word, He will always reveal a way out of trouble. Let God's word be the foundation of your life. Meditate on His promises, then will you see the picture that God is trying to reveal. Remember the way you see yourself should always line up with the word of God. Read three scriptures-reread them until the picture is very clear.

And the Lord shall make thee plenteous in goods, in the fruit of thy body, and in the fruit of thy cattle, and in the fruit of thy ground, in the land which the land which the Lord sware unto thy fathers to give thee.

The Lord shall open unto thee his good treasure, the heaven to give the rain unto thy land in his season and to bless all the work of thine hand; and thou shalt lend unto many nations, and thou shalt not borrow.

And the Lord shall make thee the head, and not the tail; and thou shalt be above only, and thou shalt not be beneath.

(Deuteronomy 28: 11-13 KJV)

Chapter 4

Keeping Your Mouth Full of God's Word

What we say will determine what we receive. Success and victory are in the mouth. If we say that we can, we have already won the battle. If we say that we cannot, we are already defeated. Therefore, we must keep my mouth full of God's word and should only say what God's word says about our condition. Anything else would destroy us:

> Death and life are in the power
> Of the tongue: And they that love
> It shall eat the fruit thereof.
>
> Proverbs 18:21

God wants our mouths to stay full of His word. For we are made in His image and likeness. The world was created by the spoken word of God. "And God said, Let there be light: and there was light," (Gen 1:3). Since we are made in His image and likeness, God knows the power of our words. If He spoke those things that be not as though they were, (Romans 4:17), so can we.

Our responsibility as believers is to imitate God in our speech. There is no other way to get results. Using our own words will never bring us out our situation. Remember that the angels only hearken to the voice of His word..(Psalm 103:20). Unless we speak His word, the angels will not work on our behalf.

We have the authority to speak to every mountain in our lives. It does not matter how big the problem is; it must obey the word of God. Everything is subject to His word:

For verily I say unto you,
That whatsoever shall say unto this
mountain, Be thou removed, and
be thou cast into the sea; and
shall not doubt in his heart but
shall believe that those things which
he saith shall come to pass; he shall
have whatsoever he saith
                    Mark 11:23 KJV

Joshua was able to cross the Jordan because of God's word. The Lord said to Joshua, 'This book of the law shall not depart out of thy mouth…(Joshua 1:8). What was God trying to reveal to Joshua? The answer is simple: keep your mouth full of His word. Do not spend time listening to the negative words of others. Make sure you are not snared by the words of others. Focus on this Book of the Law. In spite of how bad situations may look, never let it depart from your mouth. Speak the word in the morning, noon, and night.

My pastor preached a sermon entitled, "Talk your way out of it." I know that sometimes the problems of life seem too hard to bear. The storms we encounter seem to overwhelm us. In spite of our circumstances, there is a way out. You can talk your way out of it. In other words, continue to speak God's word until there is change in your situation. If we continue to confess His word over our condition, change must and will take place.

> Thou shalt also decree a thing and it shall be established unto thee: and the light shall shine upon thy ways. When men are cast down, then thou shalt say, there is a lifting up: and he shall save the humble person
>
> Job 22:28-28 KJV

Is the word of God really that important? Yes it is. This is why Satan fights us so hard. Satan does not want us to know what the word says. Notice the times of his attacks. They are either right before or after the word of the Lord has gone forth. Satan tries to keep us blind to who we are. If we can never discover who we are, we can never enlighten others on who they really are.

My son, attend to my words; incline thine
ear unto my saying. Let them not depart
from thine eyes: Keep them in the
midst of thine heart. For they are
life unto those that find them,
and health to all their flesh.

Proverbs 4:20 KJV

My son, keep my words and lay up
my commandments with thee.
Keep my commandments, and
live; and my law as the apple
of thine eye
bind them upon thy fingers, write
them upon the table of thine
Heart

Proverbs 7:1-3 KJV

What we say with our mouths will eventually get in our heart. This is the reason why we cannot speak negative words. Our words will affect our hearts. The Bible states that we should 'Put away from thee the forward mouth, and perverse lips, put far from thee (Proverbs 4:24).

If death and life are in the power of the tongue, we can either kill our vision or speak life to it. According to Proverbs 18:21, I have the authority to speak areas in my life that are dead and they must live again.

So do not give up on your marriage just because Satan has convinced you that it is dead. Speak life to it in the name of Jesus.

Do not give up on what God has promised you. Continue to speak and meditate on the promise. 'So shall My words be that goeth forth out My mouth, they shall not return unto me void, but it shall accomplish that which I please, and it shall prosper in the things where unto I sent it (Isaiah 55:11).

Sometimes our life seems so very dark. After trying all possibilities and nothing seems to work, life can look hopeless. The bills are passed due, and there is not enough money to cover them. Where is the light? The word of God is the light.

The entrance of God's word giveth light; it giveth understanding

unto the simple
>
Psalm 119:130

Keep your mouth full of God's word. Drink, eat, and do according to His word. The victory is in your mouth. Speak God's word over your life today. Where you are right now is a result of your confessions. Your confessions are what you believe. If you want to receive different results; change your confessions.

Paul said it this way: I Believed, and therefore have I spoken, we also believe, and therefore speak:

II Corinthians 4:13

Remember; keep your mouth full of God's word.

Chapter 5
Meditation Keys

We know the problem; God has allowed us to see the truth. Now it is the time to practice what we know. The word of the Lord declares in James 1:22 'but be ye doers of the word and not hearers only, deceiving your own selves."

We are to practice God's principles daily. This cannot be just a seasonal thing. Disobedience and inconsistency will not produce results. The fields are white with provisions. It is now time that we work the word of God.

When a thought comes to your mind, always examine the source. There are only two sources that you and I can receive communication from. It is from either God or Satan. Remember that Godly thoughts are never contrary to the word of God.

Therefore if we have any thoughts that are against or opposite to God's word; rebuke them instantly.

For the weapons of our warfare are not
carnal, but mighty through God to the pulling
down of stronghold;
casting down imagination and every high thing that exalteth itself against the knowledge of God, and bringing in
the captivity every thought to the obedience of Christ.
II Cor. 10:4-5

Adam received specific instruction from God. The Lord said unto Adam, 'Of every tree of the Garden thou mayest freely eat: But of the tree of the knowledge of good and evil, thou shalt not eat of it: for in the day that thou eatest thereof thou shalt surely die (Gen. 2:16-17).

Listen now to the voice of Satan in which Eve received instruction

And the serpent said unto the women, ye shall not surely die: For God doth know that in the day ye eat thereof, then your eyes shall be opened, and ye shall be as gods, knowing good and evil.
Genesis 3:4-5

What are you eating? Are you feeding your eyes, ears and mouth with thoughts and imaginations that are opposite of the teaching you received from the word of God.

God wants us to break our old way of thinking. I know it is hard to break old habits. Remember 'you can do all things through Christ which strengthen you" (Philippians 4:13). With God's strength, we can break old habits one habit at a time.

All deliverance doesn't happen instantly. Sometimes it's a process. Whatever it takes, we must make our minds up to have what His word said we could have. Never settle for less when we can have the best.

Daily Meditation Keys

1. Start your day with thanksgiving and meditation on the goodness of God.

2. Pray the word of God.

3. Listen to His preached word.

4. Speak His word over your family.

5. Speak His word over your church.

6. Speak His word over your finances.

7. Teach your children how to speak the word.

8. Renew your mind in the word.

Daily Meditation Scriptures

If ye abide in me, and my word abide
in you, ye shall ask what ye will
and it shall be done unto you
John 15:7

Behold, I give you power to tread
on serpents and scorpions and
over all power of the
enemy; and nothing
shall be any mean
hurt you
Luke 10:19

Death and Life are in the power
of the tongue: and they that
love it shall eat the fruit
thereof
Proverb 18:21

Meditation Keys

Blessed is the man that walketh not
in the counsel of the ungodly nor
standeth in the way of sinners,
nor sitteth in the seat of the
scornful.
But his delight is in the law of
the Lord: and in His law doeth
he meditate day and night

Psalm 1:1-2

Finally my Brethren, whatsoever
things
are true, whatsoever things are honest,
whatsoever things are just,
whatsoever
things are pure, whatsoever things
are lovely, whatsoever things are
of a good report, if there be any
virtue, and if there be any praise,
think on these things

Philippians 4:8

And be not conformed to this world:
but be ye transformed by the
renewing of your mind, that
ye may prove what is the
good, and acceptable,
and perfect will
of God
> Roman 12:2

But be ye doers of the word
and not hearer only,
deceiving your
ownselves
> James 1:22

For to be carnally minded is death,
but to be spiritually minded is
life and peace

Romans 8:6

Jesus said unto him, If thou canst
believe, all things are possible
to him that believeth
Mark 9:23

Therefore I say unto you, what things
soever ye desire, when ye pray,
believe that ye receive them
and ye shall have them
Mark 11:24

Again I say unto you, that if two
of you shall agree on earth as
touching anything that they
shall ask, it shall be done
for them of my Father
which is in heaven
Matthew 18:19

No weapon that is formed against
thee shall prosper
                             Isaiah 54:17

But my God shall supply all my needs
according to His riches and glory
by Christ Jesus
                           Philippians 4:19

Ask, and it shall be given unto you
seek, and ye shall find; knock, and
it shall be opened unto you
for everyone that asketh receiveth;
and he that seeketh findeth; and to
him that knocketh it shall be
opened
                           Matthew 7:7-8

And whatsoever we ask, we receive
of Him, because we keep His
commandments, and do those
things that are pleasing
in His sight
>1 John 3:22

And we know that all things work
together
for good to them that love God, to
them who are called according
to His purpose
>Romans 8:28

God turned my life around, I know He can do the same for you. His word is true. Meditate on His word. It is the key to your victory. Today is your new beginning! Do not let this moment pass you by. Today is the first day of the best days of your life. You can live again!

About the Author

Mr. Samuel Brown is a minister at Tabernacle of Praise Church, 850 Woodrow Avenue, Selma, AL 36701. He can be reached at 334-875-8630 or 334-875-7216.

To order additional copies of:

Meditating

on

God's Word

Call 334-418-0088
Or please visit our website at
www.UfomaduConsulting.com

www.ingramcontent.com/pod-product-compliance
Lightning Source LLC
Chambersburg PA
CBHW031300290426
44109CB00012B/662